I M P U L S E   T O   F L Y

Impulse to Fly

Almitra David

PERUGIA PRESS
SHUTESBURY, MASSACHUSETTS
1998

Grateful acknowledgment is made for permission to quote from:
Helen of Egypt by H.D., copyright © 1961 by Norman Holmes Pearson.
Reprinted by permission of New Directions Publishing Corp.

Cover art by Rochelle Toner, used by permission of the artist
Cover and book design by Jeff Potter/Potter Publishing Studio

Library of Congress Catalog Card Number: 98-67098
ISBN 0-9660459-1-2

Perugia Press
P.O. Box 108
Shutesbury, MA 01072
skan@valinet.com

ACKNOWLEDGMENTS

GRATEFUL ACKNOWLEDGMENT is made to the following publications in which some of these poems first appeared:

The American Poetry Review, "Ascent"; *The American Voice*, "Early" and "Pension"; *The Beloit Poetry Journal*, "Poem to My Hungry Daughter"; *Ellipses*, "Bogles Wharf" and "After Reading Jung's Thoughts on the Afterlife."

Acknowledgment is also made to the Blue Mountain Center where the groundwork for "Beatrice of the Cenci" was done, and to Yaddo, where many of these poems, including the Skinners Neck sequence, were completed.

CONTENTS

how did I know the vulture?
why did I invoke the mother?
why was he seized with terror?

H.D. HELEN IN EGYPT

P R O L O G U E

Through February snow
I come slowly into the
city. Lines of my lane

are not clear; holes
in the highway are hidden.
I pause near the

Conshohocken cliffs. Water
has frozen mid-rush
down the rocks. I, too, freeze,

unable to move, as though
the same touch that
halts a waterfall keeps me

poised, waiting for a
resurgence of the flow that
will bring me into this city.

What will I uproot? I have not
discounted the dead, the fertile
ground under graves; I

remember great curved hollows,
recesses rounded and waiting.
Sounds of a city swell and fall,

push through edicts and charters.
Sounds salvaged from Paphos rise;
I hold them gently,

as though they were eggs.

Pictures from the Air

The bulbs you pressed into a
strip of ground are still
pushing. You do not say

miracle. You used to
say it with the nuns. Now,
even when you tell stories to

the children, you try not to
talk about magic. Five years ago
you said how you felt was magic.

When the whistle signaled the
end of his shift, you flew,
really flew, you said, to meet him.

From the air you could see the
Schuylkill and Delaware form the
V of the city; Fairmount Park seemed

long and green and restful. You
saw highrises and churches and
City Hall. If you flew low enough you

could see small things like a
rowboat on the river. You have a
collection of pictures from the air;

none shows the blocks between the
hospital and your house, the five
blocks between your kitchen and the

emergency room. You wonder
what turn you missed, what change.
Was it too slow to be seen? Or

so fast that even as you came home from
the market, even before you
unpacked the bags, the milk had soured.

After the factory shut down
purple clouds began to stretch across
your skin. At night the laws of

gravity change; what falls in
daylight rises in the dark and
sways over your bed like a

canopy on shaky posts. You
tried to stop the swaying, were
trying to make the bed lie still when

the floor gave way.
It was a day of open windows when
you stood, head bowed as though

in front of an altar, and vowed to
remember how to fly.
In April even the air outside this

window is sweet. Your children
press against the fragile barrier,
push toward the outside, toward

what seems like spring. You
look for crayons or a toy to
pull them back; you

tell them stories; you
talk to them about flight, the
need for accurate charts.

A S C E N T

News item: *A woman described by neighbors as a good*
mother pushed her children from the roof of the highrise
housing project before jumping to her death with her infant
in her arms.

It could have been the sun,
a particular angle that made
the two-wheeled tricycle
glint against concrete,
the broken glass sharper, clearer,
the scattered vials sparkle.
It could have been that light
penetrating her eyes without
benefit of shield or shadow
that caused her to slump against
the brick wall and curl into herself
like a sheet of paper on fire.
It could have been a vision of her children
burning, rolling a ball through rubble,
or the sound of a truck's backfire
that signaled battle, again,
that sent her rounding up the kids and
herding them into — not safety —
the scarred hallway — she would
have to climb higher for that.
Children in front of her,
she climbed step after step from
molten center through earth's crust
to the top, to the roof, to the air.
She could have paused, then,
let them catch their breath.
Witnesses saw the children plummet,
but she watched them fly, saw each one
soar and ride the wind,
then tucked her baby under her wings
and took off.

COLLAPSE

When the building at
Ninth and Market folded
in on itself and on the
honeymooners from Spain
I knew that even when they
had first met in Madrid and
gone to have coffee at the Gijon
already the nails had begun to
lose their grip and the walls
to slant in a way that
I would not have seen but
someone could have noticed the
lean, the slope in the floors and
how the doors didn't quite close —

or maybe not. Perhaps the light
played tricks so that the cracks
slid through shadows
so that as the lovers
rounded City Hall and headed east,
as they walked toward the Delaware
they didn't feel the river breeze,
a shift in the wind, in the walls
a rolling to crest as they
strolled below holding on to
each other as though their hands
knew that at any moment
it all was about to give.

PENSION

you put up tomatoes and beans
pears and peaches so
in February you can bite into
warm pie   sweet fruit

and every month you set aside
a piece of your pay for the
unknown winter
unthinkable landscape in which

you will no longer dig

time on the job is material
cut into sleeves and collars
an hour is twenty or a hundred
pieces sewn   depending on

how old you have become
sitting in that row
humming to hush the machines

now you can't understand the
letter in your hand   the
notice that what you have saved is
lost   as though all the seeds you

planted had sunk beyond
reach of the sun   your
rule   basic and golden
become junk

already the news has affected
your vision   you can't see the
wrens at your feeder out back
and when you sit you

grasp the chair   unsure that
it's there

FIRE

Two years after her
funeral her house still sits
full of what she saved for
fifty years, right down to
the stacks of Good Housekeeping
and yellowed church bulletins,
and him, he sits in the
middle of it all on the only
kitchen chair bare enough to
hold him, drinks beer, and stares.

Today there is a pounding in his
heart like the knock on the door when
the men come by to warn him. They
knock more often now, come from
the fire station to tell him how
his house is a hazard, how he has to
clean it out.

Today he has decided to do it, to
carry it all out: the balls of
string, the rags, the embroidered
sewing satchel filled with
unhemmed pillow slips. He has been
dreaming of flames, has seen
himself asleep while dusty albums and
piles of brown bags begin to smolder.

He moves slowly at first,
lifts a bundle, kicks open the
back door, walks down the five
porch steps and across the yard to
where the garden used to be.
Trip after trip, boxes and
arms full, the walking

back and forth, the
counting of the steps takes on a

rhythm like the swaying shadows of
the willow branches as the breeze
picks up and the sun moves lower in
the sky, and he keeps on,
not stopping to sort, not to think of
what to save; it all has to go, the
all of it heavier than he ever
imagined as he hauls
out the door and across the yard.

He isn't sure how far from the porch
he walks before letting go, or
how high the pile has become
as November light leaves and the
house fades. He keeps on as though
pulled by the beat of his heart or
the sound of his footsteps. He
keeps on even after the dusk has gone.

The sun brings next morning's
conjecture, questions sent
skyward like the smoke still rising
from where the house used to be.
How tired his hands must have been
when finally he struck the match, how,
judging from where he lay, he had
not considered the direction of the wind.

LATE NOVEMBER

I am planting tulips in late November.
The books say it is too late, the frost
will get them before they've

settled in. I continue to poke
holes in the earth, ignore dead
leaves at my feet, damp cold

reaching my bones through two sweaters.
I focus on the pictures on the box; those
reds and yellows look strong enough to

make it. I press a bulb into the ground,
run my hand through my hair, lean back.
The street is quiet today in this

neighborhood called transitional,
somewhere on the scale between
fixable and not, that dot of time when

the root wavers, then reaches out or
pulls in, when the heart pauses
then beats again, or stops.

EARLY

this morning you explain why
you always arrive at the office early
you leave your house before the
voices come   they begin to gather like
a posse before sunrise   ready to
attack by dawn   you used to plan a

defense   set the clock radio to
jazz on full volume   but they
took an inside route   your
son's voice leads   sounds just the
way it did before he was shot
then a baby's cry takes over   then

the full assault   your mother from
her grave in Virginia   your father's
hoarse whisper that makes you
grind your teeth   your ex-husband's
fuck you, bitch   and the preacher
praying loud enough for a deaf god

you can't drive them back   not even
by filling the room with Coltrane
so you're out of there before they start
you set your clothes out   ready
the diner opens at four
they have a jukebox

Poem to My Hungry Daughter

1

I begin with my first
knowledge of you   my
rounded belly   you   a
curve inside   curved
rounded   warm
floating in that sea
that calls to us both
always back to the
warm salt

oh round daughter flesh
I try now to understand
how you began not to
see your self   what
evening you entered your
room to find the mirrors
cursed   raving
spitting in your face like
lunatics spewing obscenities
into the clean darkness of
a spring night

and how relentless those
voices   feeding on
yours   growing fat
sucking inside your belly
pretending to
breathe with you

2

you used to climb to the
top of anything   the
highest tree   the
roof   the balcony   you
could chin yourself
sprint through gymnastics
jump   dance   twirl   ski

you could turn cartwheels
one after the other in
the sand   your body straight
your arms strong
black braids flying   over and
over as though your
energy came from the ocean
and to try to stop you
would have been like
trying to hold
back the sea

but when that other flow
began   your woman's time
that should have come with
celebration flowers and song
arrived instead infected with
the modern litany   hold back
your woman's hips and thighs
hold back
hold back your arms and legs
hold back your cry hold
back your rage
hold back
hold back your sex your
laugh your fear
hold still   hold
back your voice   listen to

those others saying
show me   show me
how small you can become

    3

I want to say show me
what did this to you and
I'll kill it
but where to aim my fire
no simple monster
holds you captive   these
tentacles are so many so fine
you inhale them with the air
they lie between the pages
of your magazines   they
travel on airwaves   they
glow like neon   they
ride the sound of the
music you dance to   they
slink under your pillow   they
stick to the walls of your room
they hiss in your face from
the other side of your mirror

I try to imagine how it
must feel to be so
hungry your bones ache
so hungry your
hands turn blue   so
hungry that a mild
breeze blows chills through
your body   to be this
hungry for years   not because
you were born into a
starving country but because
you were born into a
country of starving women

4

I didn't see the
changing   only the
change   that first
trip home from college
you   standing in the
bathroom   body still
wet from the tub   your
back toward me   each
rib outlined   your
ribs a
fragile cage

take me back to
moments I missed   those
times when swarms of
stings sought your
skin and stuck there
I didn't see them
you never knew how
gently I would have
tried to
wash them off

5

twenty-six years have passed since
I first fed you   now we
sip coffee
sift through those years
panning for gold enough to
make an amulet to
ward off demons that
follow you from San Francisco to
Albuquerque to New York
that lurk here even now in this

warm cafe as we talk   as
Friday night happens on Hudson Street
as I reach across this small table
as though to touch you

you dream of slipping into a
sweet trance from which you
awake with full breasts   your
blood flowing again   your
breath peaceful   you tell me
how you cannot sleep   how
even in bed your heart
pounds through the night as
though your body were
running   running
and in my dream I
run after you   in the
distance you are
farther away   smaller

Impulse to Fly

for L.T.

fifty years ago
newlywed you arrived
at the corner lot   your
young heart beat
excited as a bird's
and you began to build ·
with whatever you
could find

you moved fast   your
light body propelled by
energy enough to carry
someone   one who
rode with you
his own wings broken

once   when yours were the
only sober eyes in the
house   you saw a
bird in reverse   tearing
the nest apart   flinging
twigs and string to the ground

it was then you knew you could
do everything   when
the walls began to
crumble   you shored them up
that is what life was   not only the
making   but the search for
each piece that would fit   the
search that both kept you from
sleep and led you to dream

when your husband died you
felt the sudden wrench   the
pulling away of that
weight grown onto your back
you felt it take pieces
of your spine   now you
struggle to come to terms
with your slowed pace and your

impulse to fly   you
know how to sit out the
bad days the way you sat out
storms with only a
few candles for promise

when the sky clears and the
wind calms   you feel the
stirring strong enough to
pull you up and out on your
own this time
at last to touch down
where you please

BEATRICE OF THE CENCI

The story of the Cenci family takes place in Rome during the sixteenth century. It is a horrific tale of Beatrice's imprisonment, isolation, and abuse at the hands of her father, a wealthy and powerful Count.

In the early nineteenth century Percy Bysshe Shelley wrote his play, *The Cenci*, based on the Italian papers. Because of his desire to have the play produced, however, he never clearly named the core of the tragedy, incest leading to patricide. In a letter to Thomas Love Peacock, dated July, 1819, Shelley wrote:

> *I send you a translation of the Italian manuscript on which my play is founded, the chief circumstance of which I have touched very delicately; for my principal doubt as to whether it could succeed as an acting play hangs entirely on the question as to whether any such a thing as incest in this shape, however treated, would be admitted on the stage . . .*

This poem is a recreation of Beatrice's voice as she calls out to her mother whom she has never known, who died shortly after her birth. Beatrice speaks on the eve of her execution by the Pope for the murder of her father.

Named in the poem are:

Count Cenci: Beatrice's father
Lucretia: Beatrice's stepmother
Camillo: a Cardinal
Orsino: a priest

The Castle of Petrella is the isolated castle in Abruzzi to which Count Cenci banished Beatrice and Lucretia.

◆

I don't ask
that you
come to me here
to hold me and
cry as
Lucretia and I
have done for
years   I
don't ask you to
come and be as
we are   a

voice against his
will   like my
smallest finger
against the
stone gate of
the courtyard

Mother I don't
pray you back to
this place   only
sing to me
strong
from wherever you are

oh sing to me Mother
I will climb your voice
hand over hand
high over these
robed men who
curse me

sing tonight
for tomorrow they
will cut me loose
at last to fly from this
motherless place
this place of
fathers   and
fathers   and
more fathers

♦

father-killer
they call me
is he dead
was his corpse
a lie   have I
chopped off
but one tentacle
as others wait to
wind round my
throat   what

are they Mother
were they children
were they taken from
the cradle   who

took them   what did
they know   did
they miss you   were
they yours

oh Mother   how
dark   how
long since balance of
night and day   the

Malleus Maleficarum
holds sway across
all thought   I
dare not speak of
reason   I
stand about to
lose my head   and

tomorrow
when it's done
who will say
this is what Beatrice said

◆

I will be
foam   water
wind   olive trees
roses   figs
I will be
pale as a
candle's halo or
maybe
Mother   I
will be
the flame

◆

but who is
here to witness this
Beatrice   this
one
in this time

between Mothers

this Beatrice
here   born too
late and too soon

why so near to
death do I speak of
birth   they call the
midwife witch   the
devil's maid they say
what name for the
father who
locks me day after
day in darkness   oh

Mother   how it fills
my head   the
sunless silence   the
dread

◆

a child   I
dragged my
fingers over
stone walls
tracing the
dark room   I
invented what I
saw   a
glimpse   word
seed   I
planted in
whatever garden I
could dig   what
flowers   what
monsters
grew there   what
animals   wild and
caught
came into me and
lived
unseen
like me

◆

to grow
what did that
mean to me
Mother   that
my legs were
longer   that
I came to have
breasts   that
I bled

he said I have
your face   I
could not see
he was in
front of my
eyes   and
behind my eyes
and when I
closed mine
his were
still open in
front of me

◆

how much does it weigh
the terror that
sits on our shoulders
slows our walk
makes our voice
low   covers the

sound of any song with
a rush of warning   a
signal to scream for
help when
there is none   the

roads are bordered with
bodies   who
are they   those
shells of people hanging
did they gather herbs
did they seek the sun
did they call to you

the space between
bodies is small   shoulder
to shoulder they hang
heads toward the ground
staring deep deep under
ground   Mother
answer them

tomorrow I must be among
those lifeless forms   and
who shall be the judge to
name my crime   the

Pope the holy Clement
he of the scarlet robe and

cup of gold   he anointed
holy holy holy   he
with the *Malleus* in his
hand   he of the
rack and blade

◆

the monk in
the library   what
is he reading
are your
letters there   have
they saved your
ashes in a
sacred urn   what
words   what
chants will

pull them
whole and
vital   up
again
into our hands

◆

I call to
you Mother to
hear my story
though I know
you know it
I need to
say it   for
now at last my
voice is free

perhaps my words
will stay here after me
living quietly until
the time when they
will roar   bringing
the rain that will
clean this place

tomorrow they
will cut me loose
I will be wild   I
will pull fear from
the floors and walls
roll it
thick and heavy
into the square
set it

ablaze   watch
it become ash so
light the
wind will carry it away
and people   like
animals after a storm
will shake themselves

◆

Mother do you know
who created me
then carried you away
before we could speak   what

bleak vision caused
my father to
take me from Rome to
the castle of Petrella
to the gray stone of
Abruzzi   far   he said
from ears that might
hear me   from
eyes   I could be
dead   he said   and
the Tiber would flow
undisturbed

from Rome to
Petrella   what
is the distance   how
fast can a
horse run and
when it snows and
when it rains
where are the paths
and where   where
is the candle in
someone else's window

within the moat
within the walls
of the castle of
Petrella   I am

inside a
rock   set upon a
hill where none
can reach   my
heart has taken in
the gray   this
cold solitude
at night I fear
it will give up its beat
my heart or his
must cease Mother
I will put a knife
into one or the other

◆

they say witches
turn men into
beasts
accuse them then
of making the
fish swim and
the birds fly   am

I the witch
who makes the
father kick
his daughter's door
am I the
daughter   am I
the whore

◆

there is
even in darkness
a rhythm to
my day   a beat
persistent as
my heart   will

they cut it off
will it
continue
now heavy   now
light   a
tapping   a
code

◆

the salt of a tear
has not touched
his cheek   Mother
his table creaks from
the weight of
the banquet   yet
he is not full   he

drinks a toast to
the death of his
sons   that they
may not receive his
gold   he
raises his glass in
the face of the Cardinal
and laughs

◆

and what of Cardinal Camillo
oh   Beatrice the foolish
Beatrice the daughter
who begs the priest for help
Camillo speaks my
father's name
Count Cenci   the
land you gave the
Pope will glorify our Lord
now bless yourself
forget your drunken curse
look with joy upon
your daughter's sweet
face   give thanks to god

that sweet face of which
Camillo speaks is
locked behind Petrella's
gates for none to see   I

have no society   no
suitors   no dowry
save what my father
deigns to give   and

what might that be
what might he
who drinks to my ruin
grant for
Lady Beatrice's dowry

what wish have I
for marriage   save
to escape my

father's house   but
are not all houses his
do not the city and the
church belong to him

and if I were to
sleep in the streets
do not even the
ruts in the road
belong to him

◆

now that death is
near   Mother
let me speak of
Orsino   do you
see him run
back and forth as
if to please me   do
you see how he
comes near and
whispers that he
will defend me   that

he will be my ally if I
come to his bed   he will
recant his priestly
vows   he says   he
will carry me away   he
says   if
I grant him this favor

Orsino took my hand and
vowed to plead my cause
I learned that he
says yes as situations rise
yes to the Pope   yes to
the priests   yes to
my father and
yes to me   each *yes*
enmeshed in his own
hidden plan   his
thoughts already thought
before he touched my hand

◆

Lucretia held me and
stroked my head
if sweetness were
power   if
compassion could
overcome   it is
she who would
command   that the
gates be open and
the gardens tended

a woman in the midst of
men's wars she tries to
bring peace   but she
takes his blows   Mother
she bends in his shadow
we are adrift together
holding each other
trying to remember
what we knew

and Lucretia said
husband   think of
god   think of
your soul   think
that Beatrice is
dreaming of your
death   think
that Beatrice the
gentle   long since
dead   Beatrice the
child who
never was   Beatrice
the obedient
Beatrice the beautiful
is dreaming of
your death

◆

why is he angry Mother
and if anger is
madness   when
will his end   what
frenzy drives him
why has he

burned your temple
disfigured your
face   erased
your name   oh
why   what can he

see without you
through what
shadow does he
glimpse the
moon   or even the
morning sun
burning sparks on
the Tiber

♦

avarizia
avarizia
avarizia
he says   Beatrice you
are the womb
upon which I will
build my house   my
city   my
church   and I will
lie heavily
upon you   my
hand over your
voice   and you
will have no
name save mine
avarizia
avarizia
avarizia

◆

Mother   how do I
know you walked along
this river   am I
lost   do I
invent a map   but

I hear you   even
as I hear the
sea through these
dense walls   I

am proof that
you were here   I
know you through
my own breath   I
have looked for
other tracks   I
have held my
hand against these
walls   feeling for
your pulse

◆

I hold my
head high Mother
when I walk I
stretch toward you
I don't want to
see what I see
though I've lived
only sixteen years
I am old from the
cries of the newly dead
I tell you I
hold my head high
on only a thought
my body is
gone   I have no
back   no
shoulders   I am
old in my bones that
they break
turn by turn   the

Pope rides with
outstretched palms
gold drops into
his hands   gold
my father says
here and here
take this take
land take take
say holy   take
say blessed   take
say I am forgiven
say I have given to

god   godgiven he
calls his arm
pushes the door to
my room   Mother
what do you see
Camillo sees nothing
Orsino sees his own arm
they say I should remain
daughterly   when he is
drunk my father calls me
daughter   calls me his
innocent   his Beatrice
his lovely   his
flower
his

◆

Mother my cries
overtake me tonight
but I have

laughed   I have
sung   and I
have flown high
over this house
even as my father
locked the gates
secure in his
darkness   and
I have been

beautiful   have I
not Mother   I have
walked tall in my
soft green dress   sea-
green   I have brushed
my hair until
light burst through it

and did I not wait for
love   Mother   did I
not call and
pray

◆

when I call Orsino
when I call Camillo
when I say Cardinal   what

is my voice then Mother

what does it
become   to
slip through their
ears
disturbing nothing

what air is this
that lets my
words hang and
fade unheard

I hear
howls and
sweet songs
screams and
sighs   I

see red and gold
and violet on the
edge of a blade   I

am trapped and
free   bound and
flying   my
head   shorn
sprouts serpents

◆

I was afraid to
say your name   to
light a candle in
your honor
what purpose did
that silence serve

I am not only
Beatrice   I am a
story with no
beginning   or

is there one   Mother
do you know it   was
there a once   a
one time   a
place without
this plot

am I alone
is what I
know a
secret   could
I shout it if
I had a
voice   are
there

in other
dark rooms
figures
like mine
bent
eager to
hear

◆

not softly   my
arm against his
door   I did not
walk quietly to the
edge of
his bed   I knew
how the wine
made him sleep like
death   my feet
still on the
stone   still as
stone   still I am
still there Mother
standing   look at
my arm   the curve   the
blade   my
arm curved
moon white   what
night is it   what
morning is
pending   Mother do you
see fire   does the
wall melt blade glow
who is breathing in
this room   whose
heart still beats
do flames rise through
the cellar   the
floor   is the
bed red orange violet gold
I hear howls and
sweet songs   screams and
sighs   there is no

fire   Mother   it is
cold   I am still   I am
still and cold and
stone like Petrella   I am
unmoved   do you
see me   the blade in
my hand not moving   he
will not move again
he will be quiet   I will
hear the names that
come to my lips   I
name my hair   I
name my face   I
name my arms and legs and
feet   and his are
still   now   his are quiet
and it is still   and it is quiet

◆

Mother   do you
love me   do
you love me
broken as I am
do you love my
feet   my hands
my face   do you
love me when I
hear you   and

do you love me
when I can't
listen   when I
float
blind and deaf
in water with
no current   was

it your voice in
my dream   was it
mine calling names I
don't remember when
awake

this night will
become morning
I have heard
rumors of
morning   of
sunrise   and
figs ripening

Mother   I call
to you   not to
come to me here
only sing to me
strong
from
wherever you are

Swans

Their flight is high and fast,
beyond sight until they reach here
where the Chesapeake pools into
marsh, where the quiet water
and waving grass call them
from the autumn sky, and they
circle by the hundreds,
easing down, landing, taking off,
testing, settling on the soft ripples.
People with cameras gather to
watch and wait, as though seeing,
recording, could smooth the sharp
edge of longing. Wearing their
feathers won't work, either,
this far from myth.
In Philadelphia the driver of a tour bus
pulled over to ask the way
to Delaware Avenue. It's two blocks
behind you, I told him,
only now it's called Columbus. One
night all the signs to Wissahickon Drive
were changed to say Lincoln, so that
you could be standing on the ground
you were looking for, and not know it,
not know it had a different name.
This land at the edge of the bay is called
Eastern Neck, here where the marsh
seethes with regeneration, and we
stand transfixed, watching the swans.
No one speaks. The sounds are of
gentle rustling, a stirring in the water.
Some distance from the shore, but not out
to the horizon, two swans
float back to back,
the throne, waiting.

Swimmer

A woman swimming off her boat went down.
Strong swimmer, we said, *inexplicable*.
The sun sparkled smooth bay water;   hardly
a breeze skimmed white on the warm calm blue. Who
could have guessed the frenzy below? Who can
spot madness in a clear blue eye? Currents
at odds with each other sucked her into
themselves;   this is all we know. For awhile
no one would swim, seeing holes everywhere.
Talk was hesitant, as though words, too, might
plummet to another world and haunt us.
But the tides don't miss a beat;   comings and
goings soothe;   rocking comforts. Now the bay
glistens while we splash at the edge and laugh.

HURRICANE

The hurricane won't strike here directly,
but sounds in the town have become muffled,
as they do when people are suspicious.
Foot traffic is hurried and hushed; even
the rain is falling quietly, as though
to soothe, but unnerving, like a whisper
not understood. Once we would have known
what to do — which mask to wear, the chant,
the dance to appease or terrify the
gods. Not for whimsy did the church decree
death to the wearers of masks: try it. Feel
how it is to be a panther, to run
in a storm like a panther. Wind bending
the trees would be nothing to you.

PACT

Under the curve of the
garden hose hanger the
wasp's nest curved unseen

so that when she
picked it up and walked across
the yard she carried it under

her arm as casually as she
might a light sweater and
on the way admired the

blooming hostas and lilies in
the midmorning sun and thought
of the deep green hibiscus

whose blood flowers had
startled her just that morning,
hooked the hanger on the fence

pausing to look at it as she
would regard the placement of
a painting or plant and saw the

darting and heard the drone
and knew then what she had so
freely carried. She said no

to the urge to run for spray
because the unattacked should not
attack, she said, and left,

as though that pact would hold
as though tomorrow morning
when she carries out the trash

they will not surround her and
charge, covering her chest and arms,
causing her to fling off her shirt and

run for the house, twisting her ankle,
slamming the door, as though
she won't fall onto the kitchen chair,

stretch her bare arm out on the table
and sit there, watching the fire spread
red across her pale skin.

MORNING LIST

A gentle rain falls.
The yard is early-morning lush.
I want nothing to change — I want each
blade of grass to stay and the hostas near
the porch to keep opening purple flowers.
I want not to want this.
I want to accept, like the elephant whose
last set of molars has ground down,
when it is time to die. I want to
be the gracious guest who senses
when to thank the host and depart.
But I linger in doorways.
I stay seated at table when the meal is over.
I stand on the platform and wave
long after the window with my loved one's face
has sped by.

BOGLES WHARF

we stand here at the
edge   cast
our lines into the
bay   not far from the
pier   not far from the
piling where an
osprey's nest still
holds to the top

in this sanctuary
wild swans and herons
gather   the sun burns
from orange to red then
disappears   leaving
our faces suddenly gray
and the geese a pale
black in the unlit sky

this is when we
remember everything

the first fresh
Susquehanna water   the
mingling with
Atlantic salt   the
layers   one upon the other
of gifts   as though
Gaea herself had laid in
stores for eons of feasts

now   a few
watermen dock in the slips
take stock of the crab and
oyster catch   consider the
size of the rockfish
they used to know the

predator   the quiet shadow
of a hawk's wing   the

fast splash of talons   we
reel in our lines   move
closer together   touch
shoulders as if to
brace ourselves   the
water still moves with
the tides as though
nothing has changed

Skinners Neck: A Chesapeake Sequence

1

estuary *aestus*
reached by the tides
waters swell and

recede   salt and fresh
a woman stands in the
shallows   fishing

her feet feel the
silt and seaweed   the
ridged edges of shells

she moves with grace and
balance like the heron
she knows this mixture of

river and sea   its
pulling together and
drifting apart   she

understands the cycle   how
the oysters spawn on the
full moon tide   how the

eels turn silvery in autumn
and descend to the sea to
breed and die   she knows

this give and take
birth and death
moon   menses   essence

2

the old woman picking crabs
rocks slightly in her chair
her fingers feel their way
through cartilage to

sweet meat   she
doesn't look at her hands
they work on their own

when she closes her eyes
she glides along the
bottom of the bay   she
sees the undersides   the
bellies of striped bass and
white perch

crabs swim overhead
tentacles of jellyfish and
tendrils of seaweed wave   they

are worms and serpents and
Medusa's hair   they are
her own hair unclipped

even after she opens her
eyes and leans back in her
chair   she feels her
hair float   feels it
curl up and out toward the

sky   when she licks her lips
she tastes the briny drops   the
last ones left before the
wind carries them off

3

when the winds
kick up like a
tantrum

everything is a bird

pods fly on
feathered leaves   the
marsh grass flails like
grounded herons   and

farmers' sheds give up
flocks of rakes and hoes

the old woman holds steady
even when the wind
scoops up her table and

flies away   a
hungry gull before it
nose dives into the bay

4

after the storm   when
it is safe to unfold   she
walks to her garden

leaves open lush wet green
the sun glints off
clusters of three and four

she becomes like the
mustards   four parts of
their subtle cross

girl springing from the
bay   running across
the marsh toward home

mother who opens the
door   old woman who
teaches the prayer

ageless one who turns the
wheel   she is
all of them on a

single stem   four wombs
four passages

5

the sweet laurel
four-petaled flowers from
sacred groves grows
not under a Greek sun but
here at the edge of the
old woman's garden   when

she picks a bay leaf for
soup   she calls it by
its ancient name   Daphne
as though she remembers
chewing the leaves to
awaken her poems

when thunder begins to
crack in the darkened sky
she knows to make a
wreath of laurel and
fasten it in her hair

nothing can touch her then
not even the lightning that
streaks wildly across the bay
looking for a way down

6

sometimes she
feels like the
cordgrass of the
marsh   needing roots
submerged
darkly hidden
shielded by
barely moving pools
from the abrasive air

but not always
even that tough grass
even she
cannot go on without
dry ground   days when
she stretches out and
lets the sun
warm her bones

7

the old woman can be
any bird she wants to be

she has lived that long

when she flies over the
fields of Queen Anne's lace
she sees the
wild carrots   the
conical roots below the
lacy flowers

when she rests under the
willow's long branches   she

is virgin again   weaving
baskets and wands to
summon the Muses   she is

Helice and Hecate at once
come together like the
fresh water and salt of the bay

    8

when the night is clear
the old woman studies the

stars   when a gentle rain
falls on the bay she

goes fishing   she reads the
surface churn of the

water   the tangled algae
she knows how quickly

change blows in   how
rage rises like a

tidal wave   she has seen
the wind pull a

blanket of water over
fishermen and send them

down   as though they
were an offering to

Gaea   suddenly furious
at the bottom of the bay

9

sometimes the old woman is
overtaken by a sadness that
even she cannot dispel

she doesn't gather herbs from
her garden for tea or knead
the dough for bread   she

feels that the fish would not
come to her nor the honeysuckle
give her its scent

it is as though the bay itself
were pulling away from her
taking with it the birdsongs   the

sweet mulberries   the salty fish
as though it were tugging on
her very breath   not

roughly   just firmly enough to
draw her to its shore   to remind
her to walk again into the water

10

husking the last of the corn
reading the silk by the
dimming light at dusk   she

sees a swimmer caught in
the bay's downdraft   a
leaf spinning in

spiral water   she will not
catch her breath   she
will see flashes of light as

she descends to the
core   she will
follow the glowing center of

a black fish into the
chamber of waiting breath where
her own will have already arrived

AFTER READING JUNG'S THOUGHTS ON THE AFTERLIFE

we grow more contemplative
with age   preparation

for life after time is
neither the tide nor the

beating of your heart nor
how a star moves slowly fast

through black   yet
think of a thread   of one that

sews a strange unity of dreams so
unshakable that even in sunlight

it holds together
and even in the dark

ABOUT THE AUTHOR

ALMITRA MARINO DAVID was born in Pittsburgh in 1941. She studied for a year at the University of Madrid, received a B.A. in Spanish from Dickinson College in 1963, and an M.A. from Kutztown University in 1974. She currently teaches Spanish at Friends Select School in Philadelphia. Her poems and translations have been published in various journals; her chapbook, *Building the Cathedral,* was published in 1986 by Slash & Burn Press; her first book, *Between the Sea and Home* won the Eighth Mountain Press Poetry Prize and was published in 1993. *Impulse to Fly* is her second book.

ABOUT THE
COVER ARTIST

ROCHELLE TONER was born in Des Moines, Iowa, in
1940. She received a B.A. from the University of
Northern Iowa, and M.A. and M.F.A. degrees from the
University of Illinois. In 1972 she began teaching
printmaking at the Tyler School of Art, Temple
University, where she continues to teach and to serve as
dean of the school. Her sculpture, prints, and drawings
have been exhibited nationally and internationally.
She is represented in numerous private and public col-
lections including the Philadelphia Museum of Art. In
1992 her work was featured in *Printmaking: A Primary
Form of Expression* by Eldon L. Cunningham. The
cover art is from a copper plate etching printed on
Arches cover paper.